Twenty to Ma...

Sugar Br...
& Grooms

Katrien van Zyl

Search Press

First published in Great Britain 2015

Search Press Limited
Wellwood, North Farm Road,
Tunbridge Wells, Kent TN2 3DR

Text copyright © Katrien van Zyl 2015
Photographs by Johan van Zyl
Photographs and design copyright
© Search Press Ltd 2015

Print ISBN: 978-1-78221-246-1
ebook ISBN: 978-1-78126-276-4

Suppliers
If you have difficulty in obtaining any of the materials and
equipment mentioned in this book, then please visit the
Search Press website for details of suppliers:
www.searchpress.com

Printed in China

Contents

Introduction 4

Tools and materials 6

Basic shapes 7

Basic Bride 8

Basic Groom 10

Sweet Bride 12

Sweet Groom 14

Dancing Bride 16

Dancing Groom 18

Ruby Bride 20

Ruby Groom 22

Romantic Bride 24

Romantic Groom 26

Blushing Bride 28

Proud Groom 30

Mature Bride 32

Mature Groom 34

Country Bride 36

Country Groom 38

Indian Bride 40

Indian Groom 42

Chinese Bride 44

Chinese Groom 46

Accessories 48

Introduction

A wedding cake is the most recognisable symbol of the celebration of marriage vows. Personalise it by crowning it with sugar figurines in the likeness of the couple.

These cute, comical sugar brides and grooms can be personalised by changing the eye or hair colour, or hairstyles, or dressing them similarly to the real bride and groom. Instructions for various hairstyles and facial features are on flaps 3 and 4.

Add embellishments in the same design or colour that will be used at the wedding, such as flowers, a striking tie or anything else that is meaningful to the couple. Instructions for a wide variety of embellishments are on page 48.

I have used simple modelling paste (sugarpaste/fondant mixed with edible gum powder such as CMC, gum tragacanth or Tylose) for the figurines, but you could also use chocolate modelling paste, Mexican paste, flower paste (gum paste), cold porcelain or polymer clay; work with whichever medium you prefer. The limbs and decorative items are attached with edible glue, but you could use pasteurised egg whites instead.

Beginners or intermediate cake decorators can easily make the figurines in this book. As you advance, you can add more detailed elements to your brides and grooms. This book features twenty bride and groom projects, but you will soon find that you can make many more figurines with the simple techniques described.

Detailed instructions for making a bride and a groom are given on flaps 1 and 2 to avoid repetition. Simply open the flaps out and the information will be at your fingertips so that you do not have to flip backwards and forwards in the book.

Have fun creating your own unique brides and grooms!

Katrien

www.katrienscakes.co.za

Modelling paste recipe (for 250g/9oz)

Break 250g (9oz) sugarpaste (fondant) into small pieces. Sprinkle 2.5–5ml (½–1tsp) CMC, gum tragacanth or Tylose edible gum powder over the sugarpaste, depending on how stiff you want it; the more powder, the firmer the paste. Spread white vegetable fat (shortening) on your hands and knead the gum into the paste. Knead in food colouring if the paste was not coloured before. Cover with cling wrap and leave to rest for a few hours or overnight. Always knead well before working with it and rolling it out. Add white vegetable fat if it feels dry. Roll out on a cutting mat using a non-stick roller.

Edible glue: Add 2.5ml (½ tsp) CMC, gum tragacanth or Tylose edible gum powder to 60ml (¼ cup/2¼ floz) boiled water, mix and leave to stand overnight to thicken.

Tools and materials

A **non-stick rolling pin** is used to roll out modelling paste.

A **cutting mat** is useful for rolling out modelling paste and cutting out decorative items.

Scalpel/craft knife To cut modelling paste.

Dresden tool or skewer To indent grooves, mark hair or make facial features.

Veining or frilling tool To add detail to a dress or suit.

Blossom plunger cutter To make small blossoms for a bouquet or a dress.

Small paintbrush To paint on modelling paste or to brush lustre dust on a dress.

Piping nozzle (tube) Use a no.3 nozzle to cut out small circles for eyes with the narrow end or to indent a mouth with the back end of a nozzle.

Mouth tool To indent the face to make a small mouth or eyebrows.

Toothpick Dip the end into white gel food colouring to make a tiny dot on each eye.

Gel, powder or liquid food colouring To colour or paint on modelling paste.

Dusting powder, edible lustre dust or glitter To give a special finish to a dress.

Clear alcohol To mix with powder food colouring for painting on modelling paste.

Cornflour (corn starch) Use this to stop paste from sticking when you roll it out.

Sugarpaste (fondant) Mix with edible gum to make modelling paste. Use coloured sugarpaste or mix your own colours. For flesh colour, mix white paste with ivory and pink gel food colouring, or with brown, yellow and pink food colouring. Add brown, black or more yellow for darker skin tones.

CMC, gum tragacanth or Tylose Mix these with sugarpaste (fondant) to make modelling paste and mix with water to make edible glue.

Pasteurised egg whites can be used instead of edible glue.

White vegetable fat helps to soften modelling paste.

Sugar/uncooked spaghetti sticks are used to attach limbs and heads to the bodies or to keep a figurine upright. For more support, use food-grade toothpicks or skewers; tell the recipient about the non-edible items in your figurines.

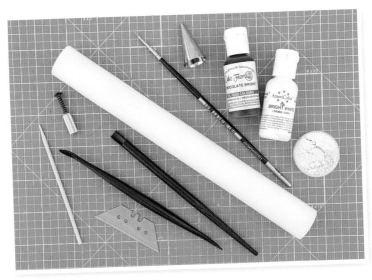

Ball: Weigh the modelling paste according to the project instructions. Roll into a ball in the palms of your hands so that any visible cracks disappear. A ball is used to make a head. Indent the ball in the centre front by rubbing your little finger over it. Roll tiny pinhead-sized balls to form a nose and eyes.

Cone: Roll the modelling paste into a ball and then a cone by pressing the palms of your hands together while rolling the paste. Use a cone to make a head, indenting it in the centre front by rubbing and pressing your little finger over it. Use a tiny cone to make ears; a large cone to make a basic dress; and a flattened cone to make your groom's torso.

Elongated cone: Roll the modelling paste into a ball and then roll it into a cone by pressing the palms of your hands together while rolling the paste. Keep on rolling to elongate the cone. Use an elongated cone to make hands for the groom by rolling the cones between two index fingers to form wrists and by flattening the wider end of each cone.

Oval: Roll the modelling paste into a ball and then roll it slightly longer into an oval to make shoes.

Sausage: Roll the modelling paste into a ball and then roll it on a cutting mat with your fingers into an elongated sausage. Use to make arms for the bride and sleeves for the groom. Fold in half to make trouser legs. To make hair, roll long and short, thin tapered sausages.

Sugar sticks: Roll modelling paste into thin sausages and let them dry overnight to make sugar sticks.

Basic Bride

Materials:

Modelling paste
  Flesh-coloured: 13g (½oz)
  Black: pinhead-sized piece
  Brown: 5g (⅙oz)
  White: 63g (2¹/₁₀oz),
  Red: 3g (¹/₁₀oz)
Sugar/spaghetti sticks
Edible glue/pasteurised
  egg white
White and black gel
  food colouring
Pink dusting powder

Tools:

Cutting mat
Non-stick rolling pin
Scalpel/craft knife
Small paintbrush
Piping nozzle (tube)
Toothpick
Dresden tool/skewer

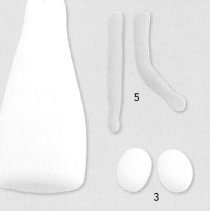

Instructions:

1 Make a head and face, using black paste for the eyes, as described on flap 1.

2 For the dress, roll 60g (2oz) of white paste into a large, thin cone 8.5cm (3½in) long. Complete, as described in step 2 on flap 1.

3 For the shoes, roll 3g (¹/₁₀oz) of white paste into two ovals and attach them to the bottom of the dress with edible glue.

4 Make the neck by following step 4 on flap 1.

5 Make the arms as described in step 5 on flap 1.

6 Place the dried head on the neck, attaching it with a drop of edible glue and leave to dry for a few hours/overnight before attaching the hair.

7 Make the hair by rolling long and short tapered sausages from the brown paste. Complete as described for long hair on flap 3.

8 Make the bouquet of roses. Roll out the red paste until almost paper thin. Cut it into thin strips with a scalpel/craft knife. Roll up the strips to form tiny roses. Attach to the hands with edible glue.

Basic Groom

Materials:

Modelling paste
 Flesh-coloured: 13g (½oz)
 Black: 63g (2¹/₁₀oz)
 White: pea-sized ball
 Red: pea-sized ball
Sugar/spaghetti sticks
Edible glue/pasteurised
 egg white
White and black gel
 food colouring

Tools:

Cutting mat
Non-stick rolling pin
Scalpel/craft knife
Small paintbrush
Piping nozzle (tube)
Toothpick
Dresden tool/skewer

Instructions:

1 Make a head and face, using black paste for the eyes, as described on flap 1.
2 Make the trousers from 20g (²/₃oz) of black paste following the instructions in step 2 on flap 2.
3 For the shoes, use 3g (¹/₁₀oz) of black paste and complete as described in step 3 on flap 2.
4 To make the jacket, roll 20g (²/₃oz) of black paste into a large, thick cone and complete as described in step 4 on flap 2.
5 Roll a pea-sized piece of flesh-coloured paste into a thick sausage. Place the sausage onto the protruding sugar stick or spaghetti to make a neck.
6 To make the shirt and collar, use the white paste and follow the instructions in step 6 on flap 2.

7 Roll out 3g (¹/₁₀oz) of black paste and make the jacket collar and lapels, as described in step 7 on flap 2.
8 Roll 10g (¹/₃oz) of black paste into two sausages, each 4.5cm (1¾in) long to make sleeves. Follow the instructions in step 8 on flap 2 to complete.
9 Make hands from a pea-sized ball of flesh-coloured paste rolled into two elongated cones. Complete as described in step 9 on flap 2.

10 Attach the dried head to the neck and leave to dry for a few hours or overnight before attaching the hair.
11 Roll small tapered sausages from 5g (¹/₆oz) of black paste and complete the hair by following the instructions for short hair on flap 4.
12 Roll out the red paste and make a tie, as described on page 48. For the buttonhole, attach one of the bride's roses (see page 48) to the groom's jacket.

Sweet Bride

Materials:

Modelling paste
   Flesh-coloured: 13g (½oz)
   Blue: pinhead-sized piece
   Yellow and brown mixture:
   5g (⅙oz)
   Light pink: 65g (2⅛oz)
   Light green: 3g (⅒oz)
Sugar/spaghetti sticks
Edible glue/pasteurised
   egg white
White and brown gel
   food colouring
Pink dusting powder

Tools:

Cutting mat
Non-stick rolling pin
Scalpel/craft knife
Piping nozzle (tube)
Small paintbrush
Frilling tool
Toothpick
Dresden tool/skewer

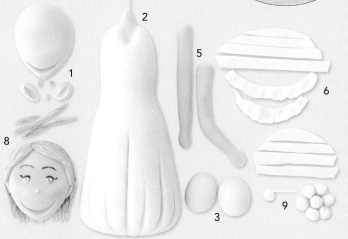

Instructions:

1 Make a head as described on flap 1 but roll it into a cone shape. Make the eyes from blue paste and paint the eyebrows and lashes with brown gel food colouring.
2 Make the dress from 60g (2oz) of light pink paste rolled into a cone 8.5cm (3½in) long. Make a waist and complete by following step 2 on flap 1.
3 Make shoes from 3g (⅒oz) of light pink paste, as described in step 3 on flap 1.

4 Make a neck as described in step 4 on flap 1.
5 Form arms and hands as described in step 5 on flap 1.
6 Roll out the leftover pink paste very thinly and cut it into strips. Roll over each strip with a frilling tool or skewer to make ruffles. Attach them to the neck and shoulders of the dress with edible glue.
7 Attach the dried head to the neck.

8 Use the yellow and brown paste mixture and make a bob hairstyle, as described on flap 3.
9 Make tiny roses with the light green paste, as described on page 48. Attach the roses to the hands of the bride with a drop of edible glue.

Sweet Groom

Materials:

Modelling paste
  Flesh-coloured: 12g (½oz)
  Brown: pinhead-sized piece
  Light brown: 5g (⅙oz)
  Light grey: 23g (⅘oz)
  Off-white: 29g (1oz)
  Light green: 3g (⅒oz)

Sugar/spaghetti sticks
Edible glue/pasteurised
  egg white
White and brown gel
  food colouring

Tools:

Cutting mat
Non-stick rolling pin
Scalpel/craft knife
Small paintbrush
Piping nozzle (tube)
Toothpick
Dresden tool/skewer

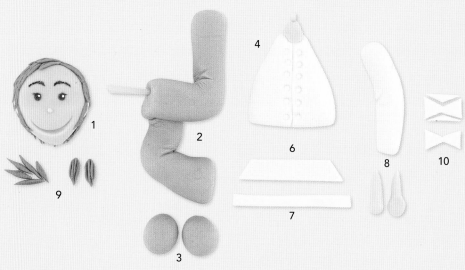

Instructions:

1 Make a cone-shaped head from flesh-coloured paste, as described on flap 1. Make the eyes from brown paste and paint the eyelashes and eyebrows with brown gel food colouring.

2 Make trousers from 20g (⅔oz) of light grey paste, as described in step 2 on flap 2, but bend each leg in half so that the groom is kneeling. Bend one leg to the front.

3 Make shoes from 3g (⅒oz) of light grey paste, as described in step 3 on flap 2. Push a sugar stick/spaghetti through the top of the back leg into the knee, protruding 1.5cm (⅔in) above the trousers. Let it dry overnight before attaching the shirt.

4 Make a shirt from 20g (⅔oz) off-white paste, following step 4 on flap 2. Indent the shirt where the neck will be attached.

5 Make a neck as described in step 5 on flap 2.

6 Make a shirt collar following step 7 on flap 2.

7 Use the light green paste and make a cummerbund, as described on page 48.

8 Make sleeves with 6g (⅕oz) off-white paste and hands with a pea-sized piece of flesh-coloured paste, as described in steps 8 and 9 on flap 2.

9 Attach the dried head to the neck and leave to dry overnight. Use the brown paste and follow the instructions for short hair and side burns on flap 4.

10 Use the leftover green paste to make a bow-tie, as described on page 48.

Dancing Bride

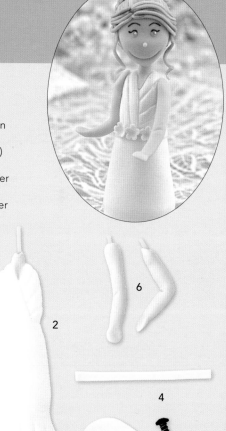

Materials:

Modelling paste
    Flesh-coloured: 13g (½oz)
    Blue: pinhead-sized piece
    Yellow and brown mixture:
    5g (⅙oz)
    White: 63g (2¹⁄₁₀oz)
    Light blue: 6g (⅕oz)
Sugar/spaghetti sticks
Edible glue/pasteurised
    egg white
White and brown gel
    food colouring
Pink dusting powder
White lustre dust

Tools:

Cutting mat
Non-stick rolling pin
Scalpel/craft knife
Piping nozzle (tube)
Small paintbrush
Small blossom cutter
Toothpick
Dresden tool/skewer

Instructions:

1 Make a cone-shaped head as described on flap 1, using blue paste for the eyes.
2 Use white paste and follow step 2 on flap 1 to make the dress. Before making the pleats, roll the cone one third of the way up between your index fingers to make a mermaid tail. Pull a Dresden tool/skewer from the bottom of the dress towards the top to make pleats in the mermaid tail. Then pull it diagonally from the waist upwards in both directions to make pleats in the bodice. Follow step 2 on flap 1 to complete.
3 Make shoes from 3g (¹⁄₁₀oz) of white paste, as described in step 3 on flap 1.

4 Roll out 3g (¹⁄₁₀oz) of light blue paste very thinly. Cut a long rectangle to go around the waist for a waistband. Cut out three small blossoms and attach them to the waistband with edible glue.
5 Make a neck as described in step 4 on flap 1.
6 Make arms and hands following step 5 on flap 1. Push sugar/spaghetti sticks into the top part of the arms to hold them straight.

Support the arms with cling wrap or small sponges so they dry in place.
7 Attach the dried head to the neck and turn it slightly sideways.
8 Use the yellow and brown paste mixture and follow the instructions for an up style on flap 3.
9 For a satiny shimmer finish, dust the dress with white lustre dust using a small paintbrush.

Dancing Groom

Materials:

Modelling paste
  Flesh-coloured: 12g (½oz)
  Brown: pinhead-sized piece
  Dark grey: 23g (⅘oz)
  Light blue: 21g (¾oz)
  White: 7g (¼oz)
  Dark brown and black
  mixture: 5g (⅙oz)

Sugar/spaghetti sticks
Edible glue/pasteurised
  egg white
White and black gel
  food colouring

Tools:

Cutting mat
Non-stick rolling pin
Scalpel/craft knife
Small paintbrush
Piping nozzle (tube)
Dresden tool/skewer

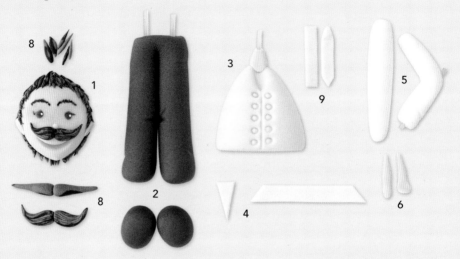

Instructions:

1 Using brown paste for the eyes, make a cone-shaped head from 10g (⅓oz) of flesh-coloured paste, as described on flap 1.
2 Make the trousers from 20g (⅔oz) of dark grey paste and the shoes from 3g (⅒oz) of dark grey paste, as described in steps 2 and 3 on flap 2.
3 Make a waistcoat from the light blue paste following the instructions for the jacket in step 4 on flap 2.
4 Make the neck using a pea-sized piece of flesh-coloured

paste and the shirt and collar using a pea-sized piece of white paste, as described in steps 5 and 6 on flap 2.
5 Roll 10g (⅓oz) of white paste into two sausages to make arms. Bend each arm slightly in the middle and attach the sleeves towards the front of the body. Push a sugar stick/spaghetti into the end of each arm and into the body. Leave to dry overnight. To ascertain the height his arms should be, place the groom in front of the bride.

6 Make the hands as described in step 9 on flap 2.
7 Attach the head to the neck and turn it slightly sideways. Allow to dry overnight.
8 Make the hair and moustache with dark brown and black paste mixture following the instructions for spiky hair and moustache on flap 4.
9 Make a tie from a pea-sized piece of light blue paste as described on page 48.
10 Place the bride close to the groom so that they are holding hands.

Ruby Bride

Materials:

Modelling paste
    Flesh-coloured: 13g (½oz)
    Black: 5g (⅙oz)
    Brown: 5g (⅙oz)
    Maroon or red: 83g (3oz)
Sugar/spaghetti sticks
Edible glue/pasteurised
    egg white
White and black gel
    food colouring
Pink dusting powder

Tools:

Cutting mat
Non-stick rolling pin
Scalpel/craft knife
Piping nozzle (tube)
Small paintbrush
Toothpick
Dresden tool/skewer

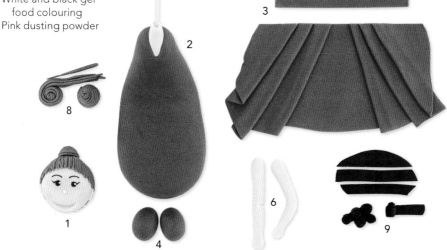

Instructions:

1 Make a round head as described on flap 1, using black paste for the eyes.
2 Make a dress from 60g (2oz) maroon paste, as described in step 2 on flap 1. Bend the cone in half with the bottom of the dress pressed flat so that the bride will be in a seated position. Push a sugar stick/spaghetti into the bodice of the dress with 1.5cm (⅔in) protruding from the top.
3 Roll out 20g (⅔oz) of maroon paste until very thin. Cut a large rectangle, twice

as wide as the bride. Pleat it, folding the pleats on each side towards the centre; cut off the top to make it even. Drape it over the skirt of the dress from the back and attach it at the waist with edible glue. Tuck it in under her bottom and fold in the pleats at the seam of the dress. Cut a piece into a long rectangle and attach it around the waist.
4 Make shoes from 3g (¹⁄₁₀oz) of maroon paste following step 3 on flap 1; attach them to the bottom of the dress.

5 Make a neck as described in step 4 on flap 1.
6 Make arms and hands as described in step 5 on flap 1. Place one arm next to the body hanging down and the other resting in the bride's lap.
7 Attach the head to the neck with edible glue.
8 Using brown paste, follow the instructions on flap 3 to make a bun.
9 Make tiny roses with the black paste, as described on page 48, and attach to the hand in the bride's lap.

Ruby Groom

Materials:

Modelling paste
  Flesh-coloured: 12g (½oz)
  Black: 23g (⅘oz)
  Light grey: 29g (1oz)
  Maroon or red: 3g (¹⁄₁₀oz)
Sugar/spaghetti sticks

Edible glue/pasteurised
  egg white
White and black gel
  food colouring
Black dusting powder
Food-safe marker (optional)

Tools:

Cutting mat
Non-stick rolling pin
Scalpel/craft knife
Small paintbrush
Piping nozzle (tube)
Toothpick
Dresden tool/skewer

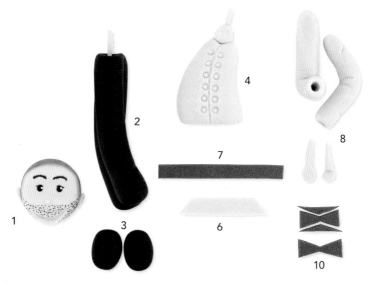

Instructions:

1 Make a round head from 10g (⅓oz) of flesh-coloured paste, as described on flap 1.
2 Roll 20g (⅔oz) of black paste into a sausage and make legs, as described in step 2 on flap 2.
3 Make the feet from 3g (¹⁄₁₀oz) of black paste and attach them to the trousers, as described in step 3 on flap 2, inserting two sugar/spaghetti sticks into the top of the trouser legs only. Place the legs in a side-lying position, bending them slightly.

4 Make a shirt from 20g (⅔oz) of light grey paste, following step 4 on flap 2. Indent the shirt where the neck will be attached.
5 Make a neck as described in step 5 on flap 2. Place the shirt on the legs and bend the body slightly upwards.
6 Make a collar for the shirt following step 7 on flap 2.
7 Use the maroon paste to make a cummerbund, as described on page 48.
8 Make sleeves with 6g (⅕oz) of light grey paste following

step 8 on flap 2. Place one arm over the body and bend the other. Make hands as described in step 9 on flap 2; bend the hand on the bent arm backwards.
9 Follow the instructions on flap 4 for a shaven head and stubble. Place the head on the neck so that it looks as if the head is resting on the bent hand.
10 Make a bow-tie from the leftover maroon paste, as described on page 48.

Romantic Bride

Materials:

Modelling paste
  Flesh-coloured: 13g (½oz)
  Green: pinhead-sized piece
  Light brown and orange
  mixture: 5g (⅙oz)
  Cream or ivory: 36g (1¼oz)
  Peach: 3g (⅒oz)
Sugar/spaghetti sticks
Edible glue/pasteurised
  egg white
White and brown gel
  food colouring
Pink dusting powder
Lustre dust (optional)

Tools:

Cutting mat
Non-stick rolling pin
Scalpel/craft knife
Piping nozzle (tube)
Small paintbrush
Toothpick
Dresden tool/skewer

Instructions:

1 Make a cone-shaped head as described on flap 1, using green paste for the eyes and brown gel food colouring for the eyelashes and eyebrows.
2 Make the dress from 30g (1oz) of cream or ivory paste, as described in step 2 on flap 1. Before making the pleats, bend the dress in half and pinch the bottom downwards so that it looks as if the bride is sitting. Push a sugar stick/spaghetti into the top part of the dress only, with 1.5cm (⅔in) protruding from the top.
3 Make shoes from pea-sized balls of cream or ivory paste, as described in step 3 on flap 1.
4 Make a neck as described in step 4 on flap 1.
5 Make arms and hands as described in step 5 on flap 1 and attach them to the body.

6 Place the head on the neck and attach it with a drop of edible glue.
7 Follow the instructions for long hair on flap 3; use the light brown and orange paste mixture. Roll the sausages for hair strands around a toothpick for curly hair.
8 Roll out the leftover cream or ivory paste until very thin. Cut a rectangle to fit onto

the bride's head. Pleat it and pinch it in the middle to make a veil. Attach it to the head.
9 Make tiny roses with the peach paste, as described on page 48 and attach them to one hand with edible glue.
10 Dust the front of the dress, veil and shoes with lustre dust using a small paintbrush (optional).

Romantic Groom

Materials:

Modelling paste
  Flesh-coloured: 12g (½oz)
  Black: 63g (2¹⁄₁₀oz)
  Brown: 5g (¹⁄₆oz)
  Cream or ivory:
  pea-sized piece
  Peach: pea-sized piece

Sugar/spaghetti sticks
Edible glue/pasteurised
  egg white
White and black gel
  food colouring

Tools:

Cutting mat
Non-stick rolling pin
Scalpel/craft knife
Small paintbrush
Piping nozzle (tube)
Toothpick
Dresden tool/skewer

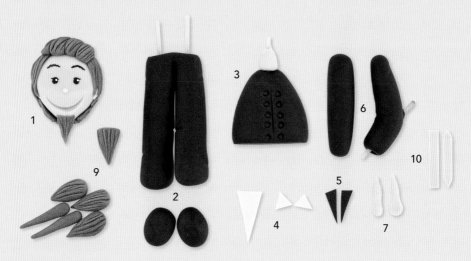

Instructions:

1 Make a head from 10g (⅓oz) of flesh-coloured paste, as described on flap 1, rolling the head into a cone shape.
2 Make trousers from 20g (²⁄₃oz) of black paste and shoes from 3g (¹⁄₁₀oz), as described in steps 2 and 3 on flap 2. Place one leg in front of the other to balance the weight of the bride.
3 Make the jacket from 20g (²⁄₃oz) of black paste, as described in step 4 on flap 2.
4 Make the neck using a pea-sized piece of flesh-coloured paste, and the shirt and collar using a pea-sized

piece of cream or ivory paste, as described in steps 5 and 6 on flap 2.
5 Use 3g (¹⁄₁₀oz) of black paste to make the jacket collar and lapels, as described in step 7 on flap 2.
6 Make two sleeves from 10g (⅓oz) of black paste, as described in step 8 on flap 2. Bend each arm slightly in the middle and attach the sleeves towards the front of the body. Push a sugar stick/spaghetti into the end of each arm and into the body. Leave to dry overnight.

7 Make and attach the hands, following step 9 on flap 2.
8 Attach the head to the body and leave to dry overnight.
9 Use brown paste to make gelled hair and a goatee, as described on flap 4.
10 Make a tie with peach paste, as described on page 48.
11 To secure the bride to the groom's body, insert sugar/spaghetti sticks into the side of the bride's body. Place her on the groom's arms and push her into his torso.

Blushing Bride

Materials:

Modelling paste
  Dark brown flesh-coloured:
  13g (½oz)
  Black: 6g (⅕oz)
  White: 63g (2¹⁄₁₀oz)
  Yellow: 5g (⅙oz)
  Off-white: 3g (¹⁄₁₀oz)
  Green: Pea-sized piece

Sugar/spaghetti sticks
Edible glue/pasteurised
  egg white
White and black gel
  food colouring
Burgundy and gold dusting
  powder
Clear alcohol

Tools:

Cutting mat
Non-stick rolling pin
Scalpel/craft knife
Small paintbrush
Piping nozzle (tube)
Toothpick
Dresden tool/skewer

Instructions:

1 Make a round head from 10g (⅓oz) of dark brown flesh-coloured paste and eyes from black paste, using the instructions on flap 1.
2 Roll 60g (2oz) of white paste into a large, thin cone and make the dress, as described in step 2 on flap 1. Place the dress on your work surface and flatten it with the palm of your hand. Bend the top of the dress up and backwards. Place a sugar stick/spaghetti diagonally through the top of the dress and make a neck, as described in step 4 on flap 1.

3 Roll 3g (¹⁄₁₀oz) of white paste into two ovals for shoes. Flatten the front end of each shoe with your finger to create a heel. Attach to the bottom of the dress with edible glue.
4 Make the arms following step 5 on flap 1. Attach them to the sides of the body, bending them forward.
5 Attach the head to the neck and allow to dry overnight.
6 Make a ponytail from 5g (⅙oz) of black paste, as described on flap 3.

7 Use 3g (¹⁄₁₀oz) of yellow paste to make a bow, as described on page 48. Attach the tail to the back of the dress and place the loops on top gluing it on with edible glue. Mix gold dusting powder with clear alcohol and paint it on the bow.
8 Use 3g (¹⁄₁₀oz) off-white paste and the leftover yellow paste to make arum lilies, as described on page 48. Place the bouquet in the bride's hands.

Proud Groom

Materials:

Modelling paste
    Dark brown flesh-coloured:
      12g (½oz)
    Black: 9g (¼oz)
    Dark blue: 58g (2oz)
    Black: 63g (2¹⁄₁₀oz)
    White: pea-sized piece

Sugar/spaghetti sticks
Edible glue/pasteurised
    egg white
White and black gel
    food colouring

Tools:

Cutting mat
Non-stick rolling pin
Scalpel/craft knife
Small paintbrush
Piping nozzle (tube)
Toothpick
Dresden tool/skewer

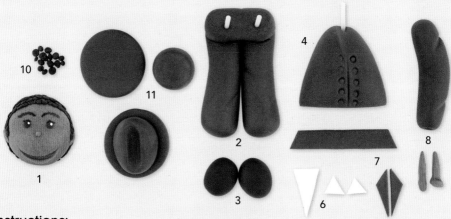

Instructions:

1 Make a round head from 10g (⅓oz) of dark brown flesh-coloured paste, as described on flap 1. Make the eyes from black paste.
2 Roll 20g (⅔oz) of blue paste into a sausage and make trousers, as described in step 2 on flap 2. Bend the top of the trousers so that the groom is in a sitting position. Insert sugar/spaghetti sticks through the top of the trousers only.
3 Make shoes from 3g (¹⁄₁₀oz) of black paste and attach to the bottom of the trousers.
4 Make a jacket from 20g (⅔oz) of blue paste, as described in step 4 on flap 2.

5 Make the neck, using a pea-sized piece of dark brown paste, as described in step 5 on flap 2.
6 Use the white paste to make a shirt and collar, as described in step 6 on flap 2.
7 Use 3g (¹⁄₁₀oz) of blue paste to make the jacket collar and lapel, as described in step 7 on flap 2. Place the jacket onto the trousers and prop it up if necessary.
8 Make two sleeves from 10g (⅓oz) of blue paste, and two hands from a pea-sized piece of dark brown paste, as described in steps 8 and 9 on flap 2. Bend the hands

so that they are flat on the ground.
9 Attach the head to the neck with edible glue.
10 For the hair, roll tiny balls of black paste and attach them to the head, flattening them with your finger.
11 Use 5g (¹⁄₆oz) of blue paste to make a hat, as described on page 48. Glue the hat to the groom's head.
12 Attach one of the bride's flowers to the groom's jacket.

Mature Bride

Materials:

Modelling paste
  Flesh-coloured: 13g (½oz)
  Brown: pinhead-sized piece
  Light grey: 5g (⅙oz)
  White: 63g (2¹⁄₁₀oz)
  Pale purple: 33g (1⅙oz)
Sugar/spaghetti sticks
Edible glue/pasteurised
  egg white
White and black gel
  food colouring
Pink dusting powder
1 small dragée

Tools:

Cutting mat
Non-stick rolling pin
Small blossom cutter
Scalpel/craft knife
Piping nozzle (tube)
Small paintbrush
Toothpick
Frilling tool
Dresden tool/skewer
Small paintbrush

Instructions:

1 Make a round head with brown eyes, as described on flap 1. Make small indents next to the eyes with a Dresden tool/skewer and mark the forehead with a knife to make wrinkles.
2 Make the dress from 60g (2oz) of white paste, as described on flap 1. Place the dress on its side, flatten the bottom and bend the top upwards. Push a sugar stick/spaghetti diagonally through the top of the cone to hold the top of the dress in a raised position.
3 Roll out 20g (⅔oz) of pale purple paste very thinly. Cut 1cm (½in) wide strips to fit around the dress. Frill the strips using a frilling tool/skewer. Place the ruffles over and under the dress, starting at the bottom and working towards the waist. Attach them with edible glue.

4 Use 3g (¹⁄₁₀oz) of white paste to make shoes, following step 3 on flap 1.
5 Make a neck as described in step 4 on flap 1.
6 Make arms and hands, as described in step 5 on flap 1. Push a sugar stick/spaghetti into one of the arms with a piece protruding at the top. Push the protruding piece into the lower side of the body to support to the arm holding up the body. Place the other arm against the body.

7 Attach the head to the neck with edible glue.
8 Make long hair from light grey paste, as described on flap 3. Curl the ends of some of the strands.
9 Roll out 5g (⅙oz) of pale purple paste until very thin. Cut out small blossoms and attach to the dress and hair with edible glue.
10 Make a handbag from 5g (⅙oz) of pale purple paste, as described on page 48.

Mature Groom

Materials:

Modelling paste
  Flesh-coloured: 12g (½oz)
  Blue: pinhead-sized piece
  Light grey: 5g (⅙oz)
  Grey: 63g (2¹/₁₀oz)
  White: pea-sized piece
  Pale purple: pea-sized
  piece
Sugar/spaghetti sticks
Edible glue/pasteurised
  egg white
White and black gel
  food colouring

Tools:

Cutting mat
Non-stick rolling pin
Scalpel/craft knife
Small paintbrush
Piping nozzle (tube)
Toothpick
Dresden tool/skewer

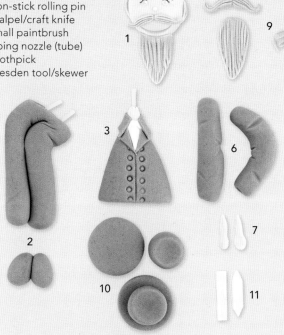

Instructions:

1 Make a round head with blue eyes, as described on flap 1. Make small indents next to the eyes with a Dresden tool/skewer and mark the forehead with a knife to make wrinkles.
2 Make trousers from 20g (²/₃oz) of grey paste and shoes from 3g (¹/₁₀oz) grey paste, as described in steps 2 and 3 on flap 2. Place the legs lying on their side and bend the top of the trousers upwards. Place sugar/spaghetti sticks diagonally through the top of the trousers to maintain this position. Make sure that the groom will be leaning towards the bride.
3 Make a jacket from 20g (²/₃oz) of grey paste, as described in step 4 on flap 2.

4 Make the neck from a pea-sized piece of flesh-coloured paste, and the shirt and collar using a pea-sized piece of white paste, as described in steps 5 and 6 on flap 2.
5 Use 3g (¹/₁₀oz) of grey paste to make the jacket collar and lapel, as described in step 7 on flap 2. Place the jacket onto the trousers and prop it up if necessary.
6 Use 10g (⅓oz) of grey paste to make the sleeves, as described in step 8 on flap 2.
7 Make and attach the hands, following step 9 on flap 2.
8 Make and attach the arms, following step 6 on p. 32.

9 Attach the head to the neck and make the hair and beard from 5g (⅙oz) of light grey paste, as described for a balding head and full beard on flap 4.
10 Use 10g (⅓oz) of grey paste to make a top hat, as described on page 48. Glue the top hat to the top of the groom's head.
11 Make a tie with a pea-sized piece of pale purple paste, as described on page 48. Attach one of the bride's blossoms to the groom's jacket.

Country Bride

Materials:

Modelling paste
    Flesh-coloured: 13g (½oz)
    Green: pinhead-sized piece
    Brown and orange:
    5g (⅙oz)
    White: 63g (2¹⁄₁₀oz)
    Yellow: tiny piece
    Pale pink: 3g (¹⁄₁₀oz)
    Green: pea-sized piece
Sugar/spaghetti sticks
Edible glue/pasteurised
    egg white
White and brown gel
    food colouring
Pink dusting powder
Small dragées or nonpareils

Tools:

Cutting mat
Non-stick rolling pin
Scalpel/craft knife
Styrofoam
Piping nozzle (tube)
Small paintbrush
Toothpick
Dresden tool/skewer
Small paintbrush

Instructions:

1 Using 10g (⅓oz) of flesh-coloured paste, make a cone-shaped head with green eyes, as described on flap 1. Paint the eyelashes and eyebrows with brown gel food colouring.
2 Using 60g (2oz) of white paste, make the dress as described in step 2 on flap 1. Indent the top of the dress with your index finger to create a neckline. Bend the dress into a sitting position over the edge of a piece of Styrofoam. Mark a line around the waist and pull a Dresden tool/skewer upwards from the waist to form pleats on the bodice. Mark random pleats on the skirt of the dress and attach dragées or nonpareils with edible glue. Push a sugar stick/spaghetti through the top to protrude 1.5cm (⅔in).

3 Make shoes from 3g (¹⁄₁₀oz) of white paste, following step 3 on flap 1.
4 Roll a small piece of flesh-coloured paste into a cone. Place it over the sugar stick/spaghetti and flatten it onto the top of the dress, attaching it with a drop of edible glue.
5 Form arms and hands, as described in step 5 on flap 1. Attach them to the sides of the body, bending the arms forward and placing the bride's hands in her lap.
6 Attach the head to the neck with edible glue.

7 For the hair, make tapered sausages from 5g (⅙oz) of brown and orange paste and glue them to the head, starting from the forehead, placing them with a side parting towards the neck. Roll a few tapered sausages and pinch them at one end to stick them together. Twist the ponytail and glue it to the back of the head, close to the neck, and let it hang over the bride's shoulder. Roll a few short tapered sausages to make a fringe.
8 Make pink arum lilies, as described on page 48, and place on the bride's lap.

Country Groom

Materials:

Modelling paste
  Flesh-coloured: 12g (½oz)
  Green: pinhead-sized piece
  Yellow and brown mixture:
  5g (⅙oz)
  Dark ivory: 22g (¾oz)
  Brown: 3g (⅒oz)
  Pale green: 27g (⅞oz)
  Pink: small piece

Sugar/spaghetti sticks
Edible glue/pasteurised
  egg white
White and brown gel
  food colouring

Tools:

Cutting mat
Non-stick rolling pin
Scalpel/craft knife
Styrofoam
Small paintbrush
Piping nozzle (tube)
Toothpick
Dresden tool/skewer

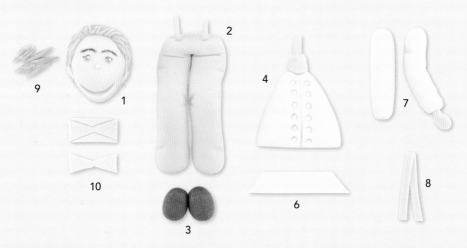

Instructions:

1 Using 10g (⅓oz) of flesh-coloured paste, make a cone-shaped head with green eyes, as described on flap 1. Paint the eyelashes and eyebrows with brown gel food colouring.

2 Use 20g (⅔oz) of dark ivory to make trousers, as described in step 2 on flap 2. Bend the trousers at the hips and knees into a sitting position over a piece of Styrofoam. Push sugar/spaghetti sticks into the top of the trousers at the waist, protruding 1.5cm (⅔in).

3 Make shoes from 3g (⅒oz) of brown paste, as described in step 3 on flap 2.

4 Make a shirt instead of a jacket from 20g (⅔oz) of pale green paste, following step 4 on flap 2.

5 Make a neck as described in step 5 on flap 2.

6 Make a shirt collar, following the instructions for the jacket in step 7 on flap 2.

7 Make sleeves with 6g (⅕oz) of pale green and the hands with a pea-sized piece of flesh-coloured paste, as described in steps 8 and 9 on flap 2.

8 Roll out a small piece of dark ivory paste and cut two long thin strips. Attach these over the shoulders of the groom to make braces.

9 Attach the head to the neck. Make hair from the yellow and brown paste mixture, following the instructions for short hair on flap 4.

10 Make a bow-tie from a small piece of pink paste following the instructions on page 48.

Indian Bride

Materials:

Modelling paste
  Light brown flesh-coloured:
  13g (½oz)
  Black: 6g (⅕oz)
  Bright pink: 83g (3oz)
  Mustard yellow: 5g (⅙oz)
Sugar/spaghetti sticks

Edible glue/pasteurised
  egg white
White and black gel
  food colouring
Pink dusting powder
Gold dusting powder
Clear alcohol

Tools:

Cutting mat
Non-stick rolling pin
Scalpel/craft knife
Blossom cutter
Small paintbrush
Piping nozzle (tube)
Toothpick
Dresden tool/skewer

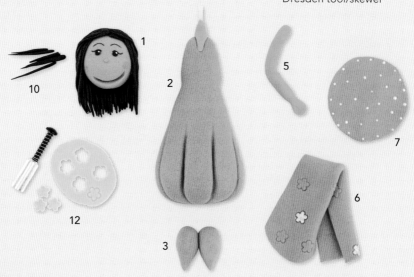

Instructions:

1 Using 10g (⅓oz) of light brown paste, make a round head with black eyes, as described on flap 1.
2 Using 60g (2oz) of pink paste make a dress, as described in step 2 on flap 1.
3 Make the shoes from 3g (⅒oz) of pink paste following step 3 on flap 1. Pinch the fronts into sharp points; attach the shoes to the bottom of the dress with edible glue.
4 Make a neck as described in step 4 on flap 1.

5 Make arms as described in step 5 on flap 1, but attach them at the shoulders only.
6 Use 20g (⅔oz) of pink paste to make a sari as described on page 48.
7 Make veil with the pink off-cuts as described on page 48.
8 Drape the sari over one shoulder and diagonally over the dress, tucking it in under the opposite arm. Glue it onto the back of the dress and attach the arms.
9 Attach the head to the neck with edible glue.

10 Make a long hairstyle from 5g (⅙oz) of black paste, as described on flap 3.
11 Glue the veil onto the bride's head.
12 Make small blossoms from 5g (⅙oz) of yellow paste, as described on page 48, and attach them to her hands.
13 Mix gold dusting powder with clear alcohol and paint the embossed blossoms on the sari as well as the flowers in the boquet. Use a toothpick to dab gold dots on the veil.

Indian Groom

Materials:

Modelling paste
  Light brown flesh-coloured:
  12g (½oz)
  Black: small piece
  Mustard yellow: 49g (1¾oz)
  Bright pink: 10g (⅓oz)
Sugar/spaghetti sticks
Edible glue/pasteurised
  egg white
White and black gel
  food colouring
Gold dusting powder
Clear alcohol

Tools:

Cutting mat
Non-stick rolling pin
Scalpel/craft knife
Small paintbrush
Piping nozzle (tube)
Toothpick
Dresden tool/skewer

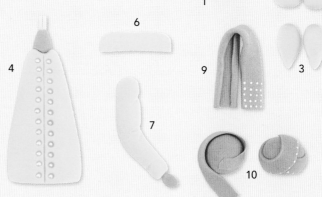

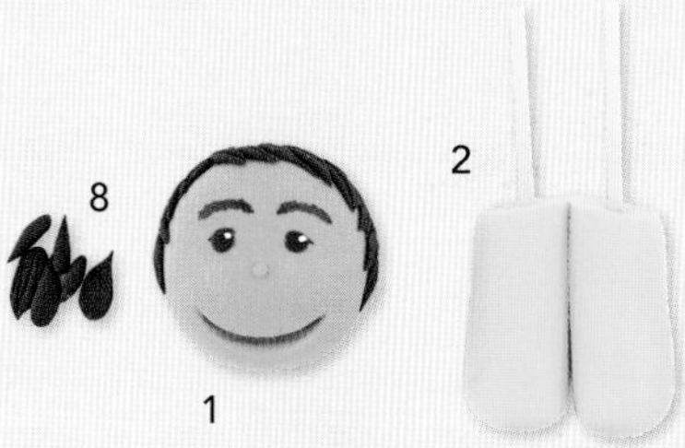

Instructions:

1 Using 10g (⅓oz) of light brown paste, make a round head with black eyes, as described on flap 1.
2 Use 10g (⅓oz) of mustard yellow paste to make trousers following step 2 on flap 2, but keep in mind that the trousers will only be 3cm (1¼in) long.
3 Make the shoes from 3g (⅒oz) of yellow paste, following step 3 on flap 1. Pinch the fronts into sharp points. Stick two sugar/spaghetti sticks through the trouser legs into the feet, protruding 2.5cm (1in) above the trousers.
4 Roll 30g (1oz) of mustard yellow paste into a large, thick cone 7.5cm (3in) long. Flatten

the cone and cut it off at the widest end. Complete by following the instructions for the jacket in step 4 on flap 2. It should be 6cm (2½in) long and will need longer sugar/spaghetti sticks for support.
5 Make a neck as described in step 5 on flap 2.
6 Make a collar from mustard yellow paste, as described in step 7 on flap 2, but cut the two top corners of the rectangle round instead of diagonally.
7 Make sleeves from 6g (⅕oz) of yellow and hands from a pea-sized piece of light brown paste, as described in steps 8 and 9 on flap 2.

8 Attach the head to the neck and make short hair from black modelling paste for the front of the head only.
9 Use 5g (⅙oz) of bright pink modelling paste to make a stole, as described on page 48. Drape the stole over the groom's shoulder.
10 Use 5g (⅙oz) of bright pink modelling paste and make a turban, as described on page 48.
11 Mix gold dusting powder with clear alcohol and use a toothpick to dab dots on the bottom edge of the stole, on the edge of the turban and on the buttons.

Chinese Bride

Materials:

Modelling paste
   Flesh-coloured: 12g (½oz)
   Black: 6g (⅕oz)
   Red: 72g (2½oz)
   Dark ivory: 3g (⅒oz)
Sugar/spaghetti sticks
Edible glue/pasteurised
   egg white
White and black gel
   food colouring
Pink dusting powder
Gold dusting powder
Clear alcohol

Tools:

Cutting mat
Non-stick rolling pin
Scalpel/craft knife
Small paintbrush
Piping nozzle (tube)
Toothpick
Dresden tool/skewer

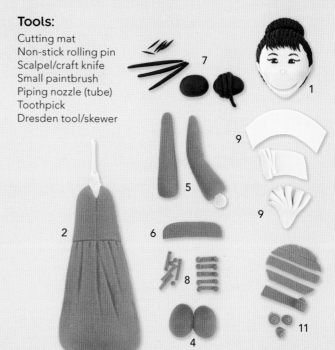

Instructions:

1 Make a cone-shaped head as described on flap 1. Make one eye from black paste. Halve it and use the two halves for eyes.
2 Roll 60g (2oz) of red paste into a large, thin cone. Mark a horizontal line right around the body two-thirds up the cone to make a waist. Mark pleats from the waist to the bottom of the dress with a Dresden tool/skewer. Mark a vertical line down the centre of the bodice.
3 Complete the dress following step 2 on flap 1 and make the neck following step 4.
4 Make shoes from 3g (⅒oz) of red paste, as described in step 3 on flap 1.
5 Use 5g (⅙oz) of red paste and make the sleeves, as described in step 8 on flap 2, then make the hands, as described in step 9.
6 Make a collar from red paste, as described in step 7 on flap 2 but cut the two top corners of the rectangle round instead of diagonally.

7 Attach the head to the neck. For quick hair, mix 5g (⅙oz) of black paste with vegetable fat until soft and sticky. Glue uneven bits of paste to the head, overlapping them to cover the whole head. Flatten the paste with your finger. Pull a Dresden tool/skewer over the paste to create strands of hair. Roll leftover paste into an oval shape. Glue the oval to the top of the head to create a large bun. Roll a few long, tapered sausages placing them from the front to the back of the bun. Roll small, tapered sausages for a fringe.

8 Thinly roll out leftover red paste. Cut five tiny rectangles for frogs and roll ten pinhead-sized balls for buttons. Glue the buttons and frogs to the front of the dress.
9 Use 3g (⅒oz) of dark ivory paste and make a fan, as described on page 48 and place it under the bride's hands.
10 Mix gold dusting powder with clear alcohol. Paint gold scrolls on the bottom of the sleeves and paint the buttons and frogs as well as the top of the fan gold.
11 Make tiny roses from red paste, as described on page 48; attach them to the bun.

Chinese Groom

Materials:

Modelling paste
    Flesh-coloured: 12g (½oz)
    Black: 6g (⅕oz)
    Red: 85g (3oz)
Sugar/spaghetti sticks

Edible glue/pasteurised
    egg white
White and black gel
    food colouring
Gold dusting powder
Clear alcohol

Tools:

Cutting mat
Non-stick rolling pin
Scalpel/craft knife
Small paintbrush
Piping nozzle (tube)
Toothpick
Dresden tool/skewer

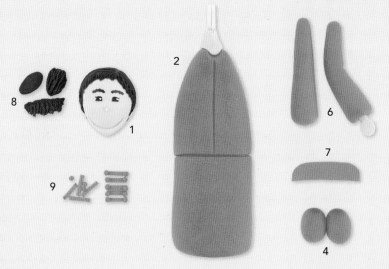

Instructions:

1 Make a cone-shaped head as described for the Chinese bride (step 1, page 44).

2 For the coat, roll 70g (2½oz) of red paste into a thick sausage, 9cm (3⅔in) long. Taper one end into a point and flatten the body slightly. Complete by following the instructions for a bride's dress in step 2 on flap 1.

3 Mark a horizontal line right around the middle of the body for the waist. Mark a vertical line down the centre of the body from the neck to the waist.

4 Roll 3g (¹⁄₁₀oz) of red paste into two ovals. Attach them to the bottom of the body with edible glue to make shoes.

5 Make a neck as described in step 5 on flap 2.

6 Use 10g (⅓oz) of red paste to make sleeves, as described in step 8 on flap 2, then follow step 9 to make hands.

7 Make a collar from red paste, as described in step 7 on flap 2 but cut the two top corners of the rectangle round instead diagonally.

8 Attach the head to the neck. Make quick hair from 5g (⅙oz)

of black paste following the instructions for the Chinese bride (step 8, page 44), but omit the bun.

9 Thinly roll out the leftover red paste. Cut out seven tiny rectangles to use for frogs and roll fourteen pinhead-sized balls to use for buttons. Glue the buttons and frogs down the front of the body.

10 Mix gold dusting powder with clear alcohol. Paint the buttons and frogs and dab dots around the bottom of the sleeves.

Accessories

Mix and match the modelling paste accessories from different projects to suit the real-life couple.

Roses: Roll paste on your cutting mat with a non-stick roller until almost paper thin. Cut into thin strips with a scalpel/craft knife. Roll up the strips to form tiny roses. Attach to the hands of the bride with edible glue/egg white to form a bouquet.

Arum lilies: Roll tiny sausages from yellow paste. Divide 3g (¹⁄₁₀oz) of white paste into smaller pieces and roll into cones. Flatten and roll each cone around a small yellow sausage, attaching the overlapping side with edible glue/egg white. Make an elongated cone from green paste; mark straight lines with a knife like a bunch of stems. Glue arum lilies to the stems.

Blossoms: Roll out 5g (¹⁄₆oz) of paste. Cut out small blossoms with a blossom cutter and attach them to the hands of the bride/her dress/hair with edible glue/egg white.

Veil: Roll out paste very thinly. Cut a rectangle to fit onto the bride's head. Pleat the rectangle and pinch it in the middle to make a veil. Attach it to the head.

Handbag: Roll 5g (¹⁄₆oz) of paste into a ball and flatten slightly. Cut out a small rectangle with a craft knife/scalpel. Roll out the leftover paste until very thin and cut out a small triangle. Glue the triangle over the top of the rectangle and attach a small dragée to the tip of the triangle.

Bow: Roll out 3g (¹⁄₁₀oz) of paste. Cut out two small rectangles with a craft knife/scalpel. Bend the ends of one rectangle towards the middle to form a loop on each side. Roll a tiny piece of paste into a ball and attach it to the middle of the bow. Cut the second rectangle in half and cut one end of each smaller rectangle diagonally to make the tail of the bow. Attach the tail to the back of the dress and place the loops on top, gluing it on with edible glue/egg white.

Fan: Roll out 3g (¹⁄₁₀oz) of paste and cut it into a curved rectangle. Pleat the rectangle from one side to the other and pinch the bottom pleats together to form a fan.

Sari: Roll out 20g (²⁄₃oz) of paste. Cut the paste into a rectangle 20cm (8in) long and emboss the rectangle by lightly pressing a blossom cutter into the paste.

Tie: Roll out paste and cut it into a thin rectangular strip to form a tie. Fold back two corners of the strip to form a triangle at the top of the tie and cut off the opposite two corners to form the bottom of the tie. Attach the tie to the groom's shirt with a drop of edible glue/egg white.

Bow-tie: Roll out modelling paste until almost paper thin. Cut it into a rectangular strip and cut away a triangle from the top and bottom of the rectangle to make a bow-tie. Attach it to the shirt with a drop of edible glue/egg white.

Cummerbund: Roll out paste very thinly. Cut out one long rectangle 10cm (4in) long and attach it around the waist.

Braces: Roll out paste and cut two long thin strips. Attach over the groom's shoulders.

Hat: Roll out 10g (¹⁄₃oz) of paste until thin. Cut out a circle. Roll a small thick sausage, slightly narrower than the circle and glue it to the circle with edible glue/egg white. Indent the top, sides and bottom of the hat with your finger. Glue the hat to the top of the groom's head.

Top hat: Roll out 10g (¹⁄₃oz) of paste until thin. Cut out a circle. Roll a medium-long sausage, slightly narrower than the circle, and glue it to the circle with edible glue/egg white. Indent the top and bottom of the hat with your finger. Glue the hat to the top of the groom's head.

Stole: Roll out 5g (¹⁄₆oz) of paste until very thin. Cut out a thin rectangle 10cm (4in) long. Fold the sides inwards to create a softer edge that looks like fabric. Drape over the groom's shoulder.

Turban: Divide 5g (¹⁄₆oz) of paste in half. Roll half the paste into a ball and flatten it onto the groom's head. Cut a long, thin rectangle from the leftover paste. Attach one end of the rectangle to the centre front of the flattened ball and drape the rectangle around the flattened ball to cross back over at the front. Attach it with edible glue/egg white.